Eighteen Poems
and
Two Short Stories

William Duxbury

DEDICATION
For Agnes

Contents

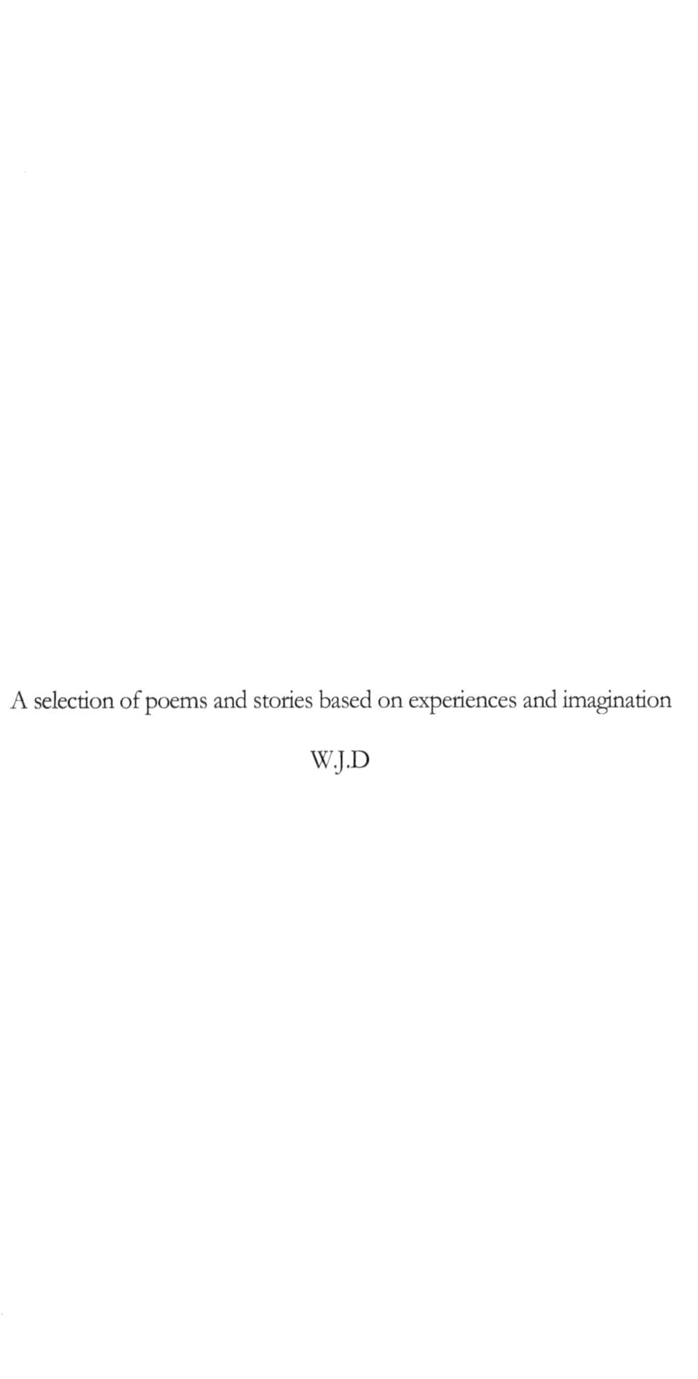

A selection of poems and stories based on experiences and imagination

W.J.D

Foreword

My father was a simple man, not in mentality but needs.
Born December 1st, 1935, raised in the wreckages of World War II bombed-out
houses in the East End of London.
The eldest of 4 children who yearned for freedom from his alcoholic father
and to finally have something of his own.

Moving temporarily from London to "the sticks" of Norwich as a farmhand,
doing his national service, teaching himself photography, working for an expert stamp collector,
working 100 jobs until settling as a school keeper while married to my Mother, Agnes and being the
best father he could be to me, his only son and 20 or so years later, Grandfather to his 3
Granddaughters Baylea, Piper and Jazmyn.

As I said, he was a simple man but of strong values and morals.
He took no shit and stood by his opinion and sound old-school judgement.

His personality was jovial, he'd amuse us with daily puns and funny stories from his many life
experiences that would fill an afternoon visit to my parent's home.

As well as his jokes, was his skill to pen rhymes and quick quips in a short matter of time.

This book is a collection of poems my father had penned over the years.

Originally a short-run release via his late brother in-laws printing press
for about 50 copies back in 2001.
I now want to release my father's words, rhyme, and life into the digital age and share
with all that knew him, or not, from these pages.

Taken from us quickly and too early by Covid-19 on the 15th March 2021,
this book of 18 poems and 2 short stories is released to honour
my father, friend, and influencer to my many interests, William Duxbury.

We miss you so much.

Love you Dad

Paul Duxbury

A FEW WORDS
1963

A thousand thoughts in my mind
To say I love you true.
A thousand words upon my lips
To say I really do.
But I get so tongue-tied
I can only say a few.
And these few words, my darling are
"I always will love you."

WITHOUT YOU
1963

It is cold in the shadows.
Cold and lonely too.
It is the same in the sunshine
When I am without you.

Many small, though wonderous things happen
To start each day anew.
Yet I do not appreciate these things
When I am without you.

Patterned frost on a window pane.
Green grass bathed in dew.
How can these wonderous things be shared
When I am without you.

DO YOU REMEMBER?
1964

Do you remember the day we first met?
You know, I was really quite shy.
And without a doubt, when I asked you out
No one was more happier than I!

Do you remember when we first held hands?
Oh! The ecstasy of your gentle touch!
You were so divine. And you were mine!
Yes. I loved you ever so much.

Do you remember when we first kissed?
I trembled with desire!
Your sweet caress. Such tenderness
Filled my soul with fire!

Do you remember that night we both cried?
Were we never to meet again?
Did you realise that the tears in my eyes
Came from my heart in pain?

FOOLISH ME
1964

I knew it was going to happen
But I just shut my eyes.
I was just clutching at a straw.
How can a fool be wise?

And now that you have left me
I have a broken heart
And I ask myself the question
Why did we have to part.

To be forewarned is to be forearmed
But there was nothing I could do
And all I can say, my darling,
Is that I still love you.

I AM LOST
1963

Once I was akin to a sturdy oak.
Not thriving on the sun above
But growing stronger every day
In the warmness of your love.

But when you said you did not love me
It was like darkness overhead.
No longer your love to succour me
But drained of pride and strength instead.

So much I wanted to protect you.
Encompass you in my arms so strong.
To hold you gently in my hands.
I was so foolish to do wrong.

A tempestuous storm overtook me.
Lightening flashing made me blind.
With thunderous words I killed your love.
My God! I was so unkind!

And as like the Autumn wind
That plucks the leaves from a tree,
Leaving the arms so gnarled and bare
So the same has happened to me.

Now I am a weeping willow
Drooping with age beyond my years
And the river that flows beside me
Is a river of my tears.

As I shamefully hang my head.
Crying bitter tears of regret
Hoping, in the darkness groping
Is there a chance of forgiveness yet?

YOU
1964

My heart stood still and let out a cry
When you said to me goodbye.
I don't want to live now. Just let me die.
Because I have lost you.

I wandered down a lonely lane
Trying hard to forget the pain.
But found it hard to break the chain
As I kept on thinking of you.

The music of birds singing in the trees.
Butterflies dancing on the breeze.
The sweet smell of flowers and many more things than these
Kept reminding me of you.

As the tears from my cheeks did fall
Into the stillness of a pool
I saw not the image of a fool
All I saw was you.

MISSING YOU
1964

Endlessly, I search for you
All I hear is the wind a-sighing
And as raindrops touch my cheeks
I know that you are crying.

Sometimes I reach out to touch you.
Just a tender sweet caress.
Suddenly a cloud comes between us
And I am alone in the darkness.

Although I know you are in Heaven
I keep on searching for you
And my search will come to an end
When I reach Heaven too.

DEPRESSION
1964

As like the waves that ebb and flow
So similar am I.
One moment I advance to enjoy Life's glow,
The next I recede into depression to lie.

Life's problems are but shells upon a vast beach
And the Tides of Experience do cover some.
And as others you have yet to reach
So you have to cover these too, as they come.

Will I, like the incoming tide
That slowly but surely conquers the shore,
Conquer Life's problems or will I slide
Into depression for evermore?

Roffey House, in Horsham was a Rehabilitation Centre.
I was there for three months.

HELP ME LIVE
1964

I was part of the Flotsam of Humanity
That came to Roffey's door.
"Take me. Help me" was my plea.
"Please help me feel secure."

Yet with distrust I was fraught.
What really could be done.
But to help oneself, I was taught,
Is half the battle won.

I was taught to face up to life,
Guided what path to follow.
Helped to free the stress and strife.
There is more to life than sorrow.

Yes, I was helped, though found it hard
To accept what I had to do.
Roffey, you have my deepest regard
And I humbly say.... "Thank you."

Now the time has come to say goodbye
And from you I must part.
And although you do not see me cry
The tears are in my heart.

To all of you who are here
Roffey has a lot to give.
But you must have great faith, not fear.
Have faith, have courage... and live.

The MAD magazine, which is still published today (2000), has a cartoon strip called Spy vs Spy.
Part of the header incorporates a morse coded message.
The cartoonist's name is PROHIAS.

FRAY BENTOS SOLVES SECRET!!
1956

In reference to MAD mag. Number Twelve
One day I did into it delve.
Reading it was like being in Seventh Heaven
Until I came to page Number Seven

For under the Heading of SPY-v-SPY
Was something strange that caught my eye.
There I saw blots and splashes
Which somehow looked like dots and dashes.

Then suddenly it hit me (Ouch!) of course!
It must be a secret message written in Morse!
Shaking with excitement I set to find out
What the message was all about.

"-•••" turned out to be "B"
But "-•---" Really got me!
I wondered, was the code in a foreign language?
(During this time I was eating a sandwich).

What was "-•---"? I felt the biggest of flops
When a piece of corned beef fell from my chops.
It landed, spot on, on the very last dash
And my teeth no longer in despair did I gnash

For "-•---" turned out to be "-•--" and why!
It turned out to be the letter "Y"
So after all it was a printer's hash
Which caused there to be an extra dash!

The rest was easy (what a brilliant brain I has)
For the full message now read "BY PROHIAS"

A NUDE AWAKENING!
1958

About three or four times a week
When I am feeling low
I usually go and watch
A luscious striptease show.

Now I have always thought
This a normal thing to do
Until I saw a psychiatrist's report
In a newspaper issue.

I don't know if the theory was Adler, Freud or Jung
But it stated that if a person, when as a child so young
Did not see it's mother in the bathroom, nude
Then it could grow up and do things regarded to be crude.

Looking back on my childhood,
It fills me with gloom.
But I blame my plight on the L.C.C
Because we never had a bathroom.

*A friend of mine knew a chap who worked on the meat counter
of a supermarket. One day, in the back room, this chap removed the bone
from a leg of meat... and shagged it!*

*The name is not real. Neither did he have an accident.
So much for poetic licence...*

MEATUS COPULI
1964

Overcame with sexual desire,
With cock a-throb and balls of fire,
The butcher boy, Samuel Spicer
Approached with lust the meat slicer.

His eyes aglaze like a glutton
For thereupon lay a leg of mutton.
He couldn't care a fuck. He was a sinner
Yet he cared a fuck for someone's dinner.

And so with his dick deep inside
He began a meaty ride.
But with legs a-tremble and arse a-twitch
He accidently kicked the switch.

Now no more meat will he serve
Having lost his sexual nerve.

A PANEFUL EXPERIENCE
1965

I awoke early one morning
To a sound from the window cill.
Was it an early bird heralding the dawn,
Breaking the silence so still?

I saw a misty outline
Moving to and fro.
It was the sweet little kitten from next door,
Locked out in the snow.

It mewed a pathetic cry,
Its paw upon the glass
So I gently lifted up the window
And kicked it up the arse.

LIFE
1978

I hear Life on all it's frequencies.
I give forth on Life with tongue eloquent.
I perceive Life with vision keen
Yet am deaf, mute, blind without Life's Element.

I wrote this poem for OXFAM but did not send it.

A CHILD'S WISH
1965

What treats for Christmas do you visualise,
Will your table be laden with goodly fayre?
Will you see children's eyes sparkle with delight?
Will Father Christmas answer their prayers?

Will you see this child with hunger in it's eyes
Wishing a pathetic wish.
Hoping for a small bowl of rice
Or perhaps a piece of fish?

Will you help this child to fulfil it's need?
Will you a present give?
To let it realise humanities creed.
Which is the right to live.

THE BOMB
1957

Humanity, in antlike activity, is scurrying about in every direction.
Believing it is living Life to a planned perfection.
But why plan? for do you not dread
That in a seconds time you could be dead?
For it is not by God's Hand that you draw breath
But by Mans' finger hovering o'er the button of Death.
One press and you are gone.
Exterminated by THE BOMB.

You there, teenager, so happy at play.
How do you plan your life each day?
By listening to records and doing the Twist.
Making sure there is nothing in life that you've missed.
Twisting to the latest in fashion and song.
Do you twist at the mention of THE BOMB?

You courting couples with your plans and dreams
And problems of how by the means
You can save so much a week to put on the side'
House hunting, H.P. your minds are occupied.
So much to get. Where's the money coming from?
What is the cost of living with THE BOMB?

Workworn husbands, haggard wives
How do you plan to live your lives?
With fags and booze and TV sets,
Up to the eyes in kids and debts.
Scraping the barrel to make both ends meet.
Isn't living an impossible feat?
Or perhaps you think life is grand
With everything going as you planned?
You have a car, a fridge, a washing machine.
'Roses round the door', isn't life serene?
Ambitions realised, what more is there to find?
Have you realised what is meant by having peace of mind?
Are you so very sure that nothing can go wrong?
Have you realised your ambition regarding THE BOMB?

Hi there, cool cats. Hi there, chick.
Solve all your problems. Become a Beatnik.
Why worry about life. What's to be reckoned?
Live life to the full. You could be dead in a second!
Why bother to wash. Why comb your hair.
It's a gasser, man, why have a care!
Just listen to jazz, make love, sleep and eat.
This is the life, man. Real cool. Real beat.
This is the way, man, to go along.
Who gives a shit about THE BOMB!

You business tycoons, you millionaires,
Living rich, what are your cares?
Chauffeur-driven cars, a house or two.
Is there nothing to worry you?
Ah! You have a pain, you do feel ill.
Quick, to Harley Street for a stomach pill!
Oh sweet relief! Now to the West End.
"To the club, James." A few quid to spend.
Tinkle of glasses, "Cheers, Sir John."
Have you ever thought of toasting to THE BOMB?

You poets and painters who talk earnestly
Of Shelley, Van Gogh and Annigoni.
You, who understand life, do you see to the fore
A vision of a nuclear world war?
This globe of ours, fountain of art and verse
Could become a scarred, charred sphere in the universe.
So although you talk of Cézanne and Byron
Do you ever talk about THE BOMB?

O Preachers of Christ. O Men most Pious
Who speak of our Lord, The Almighty, The Highest.
Who tell us there is One above
Who is warm, pure, gentle as a dove.
Who tell us to pray, the Lord will answer our call
And will come from above to save us all.
Do you know there is another Almighty above.
Up there in the Heavens but not filled with love
But filled with hate and a terrifying power
Waiting for Mans' call, waiting for the Hour.
And He will answer with a voice most strong.
Do you pray about THE BOMB?

You politicians, who sometimes talk so foolishly
How far in the future can you see?
When at your peace talks do not be too clever
Do not press the button! Never! Not ever!
Great Nations, are you not satisfied
To live together in friendship, side by side?
To help each other as arises the need
Instead of bickering with jealousy and greed?
So you politicians with all your aplomb,
Please, please do not set off THE BOMB!

You scientists with powers so great
Come tell us now, what is our fate?
You keep making tests in the search for
A mightier deterrent against a world war.
In making these tests are you sure its alright.
Are you sure there isn't an insidious blight
Contaminating our bodies. Are you sure?
And if nameless horrors we do endure
Will the children of future generations
Be terribly transformed by atomic mutations?
One thing to be sure of, which cannot be deferred from.
It was you who raped science and gave birth to THE BOMB.

PAYING THE PRICE OF STAMPS
1975

The old man sat in his Counting House
Counting up his stamps
When he looked out of the window
And saw a couple of tramps.

"Why not?" he thought, "It's Christmas"
And went to the door with glee.
One of the tramps held out his cup
And gave the old man some tea.

That night the old man lay down too sleep,
His blanket, a coat worn thin.
His mattress, a sack of stamps.
His pillow, an ink wash tin.

At last he fell into a frozen slumber.
But suddenly awoke with a fright
For there was a glow on the office wall,
And the town hall clock struck midnight.

"Who… Who is there?" the old man cried.
"How did you get in?"
"I am the Ghost of Christmas Past!'
And the old man swooned back on his tin.

He lay there in a daze,
His face as white as death.
The ghost gave him the kiss of life,
Up his arse, having smelt his breath.

Recovering, the old man asked
"Why are you visiting me?"
"To show you your past sins,
Rise, and you shall see."

They went to a Council flat
And saw a figure bent, and frowning.
"Why!' the old man said.
"It looks like Mrs.Browning."

"Right first time!" the ghost replied.
"Her Christmas has been sparse.
You paid her a lowly wage
And rated her low class."

"It's not my fault! It's not my fault!"
The old man began to squirm.
"It's not my fault! It's not my…"
He was back in the squalor of his firm.

"What a weird dream that was!" he said
With a mixture of relief and dread
And laid down to sleep once more
With his coat pulled over his head.

And once more he did awake,
This time from a troubled sleep
To see the Ghost of Christmas Present
And his arsehole farted 'Peep'

The ghost held out his bony hands.
Chains rattling with an echo.
"Come. Take my hand" he said.
"Let's go and have a dekko."

This time they went to Bethnal Green
To the home of Bill Duxbury.
"Look at this poor chap!" The ghost did cry
And the old man said "Dearie me!"

"Yes!" continued the ghost
"He really does do well
Putting up with your sarcastic remarks
And your dirty body smell."

"What about him!" The old man cried
"Writing on a toilet roll core
Sarcastic words about economy measures
And going through my office drawer!"

"Shut your face!" The ghost replied.
"You're the one who is on trial!
You want to give your workers a square deal
And give it with a smile!"

"No more! No more!" the old man begged.
"Will you please, take me back!"
Upon which he did wake,
Having fallen off his sack.

"I really must try to get some sleep.
Tonight I've had it rough"
He thought, wiping his sweating brow
With a snot encrusted cuff.

He laid down his head, so tired,
Yet fearing to close his eyes
When suddenly he gave a start.
What were those mournful cries?

"I am the Ghost of Christmas Future!"
Said the apparition at the foot of his bed.
"Come with me a year hence
And see what your sins have bred!"

They were looking down upon a scene
Of albums filled with stamps so rare
And the Devil was the auctioneer
Casting Souls into his snare.

The old man gasped in horror.
Recognising faces of old.
This was the price one paid for greed
And suddenly he went so cold.

For there was a figure in the crowd,
One, he could not exactly place.
"Who…is that?" his voice quavered
"Who is the one..... without a face?"

"Stay a while" the ghost replied
"And you shall see some more"
Whereupon the figure fell
And lay unmoving, on the floor.

Those around stripped off its clothes
And left it lying on its back.
Its skin was grimed with dirt
And the Devil auctioned "A PUNY BLACK!'

"And now, my friend," the ghost did say
Gripping the old man's shoulder, hard.
"The answer you seek is the next scene."
And it changed to that of a graveyard.

The old man stumbled along,
Suddenly aware he was alone,
Falling over unkempt graves.
Here and there, a human bone.

And yet he fell again once more
And this time did not rise
But wearily lifted his head
And the answer put terror into his eyes.

For thereupon a headstone new
Was a name he knew so well.
The Devil's stamp upon his soul.
His passport to the depths of Hell.

He clawed at the name thus engraved
Breaking fingernails and skin
And awoke to find he had scraped
'Ink Wash' off the tin.

He looked at his watch. It said 7.00 am.
Daybreak was lighting the room.
Confidence flowed through his being
And washed away the gloom.

"What silly old dreams, they were!" he mused.
"I must keep off the pickles and cheese."
And by way of ablutions, scratched his head
And killed a couple of fleas.

Therefore, unlike Ebeneezer Scrooge
The old man will never learn
That for every kind deed willingly done
There is a ten-fold return.

*I am a Schoolkeeper and keep a Job Request' book
in the Teachers staffroom.
A teacher, Mr. James Allen, made the following entry
as the door closer on his classroom door was hanging off.*

Following his poem is my response.

DOOR CLOSER
29-4-99

Oh Mr. D. I have a problem with my door.
The screws keep falling on the floor.
The door, it will not shut.
Some screws we need to put
In very tight.
You may have to use all your might.
Forever grateful I will be
When a new door I do see.

Cheers James.

James, in response to your request
I will try my very best.
From a range I will choose
And may have to use longer screws.

One thing, of which I am sure
You will not get a new door.
So in the end, as you can see
It will be repaired.

Signed Mr. D.

Two Short Stories

A SLICE OF BREAD

THE DISBELIEVER

A SLICE OF BREAD
1964

Tony Arnold stood at the Y.M.C.A dining room counter, hungrily eyeing the pile of bread and butter from which the residents were served.

Having eaten the three slices which were issued with his breakfast he now wanted three more to save for dinner. They were not to be eaten with his dinner but to be his dinner owing to lack of funds. He thought of his last good dinner of a week ago, roast beef, baked potatoes and green peas and his mouth watered at the memory of it. He thought of his dinner of the last few days, bread and marmalade and his eyes watered at the misery of it.

It had been easy to get the bread for yesterday's dinner for he had managed to whip nigh on half a loaf from the pile as the cook had turned her back for a second. Today, he would have to ask for bread as being later than usual for work did not afford time to repeat yesterday's procedure. "Excuse me." he said, in Oliver Twist fashion, "Please could I have some more bread?" Even though she was myopic and her glasses were coated with chip fat, Miss Scringe, the cook, could see the pallor of his cheeks and her heart went out to him. Seeing it was too fatty, he returned it and repeated his request. She gave him four slices.

Unfortunately, this action was observed by Saunders, the hostel spy, who was disguised as a human being.

Reverting back to his true self, a vulture, Saunders perched on the back of a chair, preened his feathers and pecked at his arse, cackling "Aha! The Grand Llama will soon get to the bottom of this!" Then he flew to the door.

Sam Larmer, the general secretary, was sitting in his sumptuous office, working out more fiddles to enable him to run his car more cheaply. And of course, the new roof rack had to be paid for. His train of thought was interrupted by a peck on the door. "Come in" said the broad Irish rogue in his broad Irish brogue. Upon entering, Saunders immediately prostrated himself into the plush axminster carpet.

"Get up, you fool!" shouted Sam. "I can't afford to have your beak wearing out the carpet. We are in the red as it is, what with that bastard Duxbury owing us fifty quid in back rent. Now what do you want?" "Oh Master, I saw one of the cooks give a resident extra bread". Actually, owing to his speech impediment, it took him quite a while to say this and for me to write it as he said it would have entailed about three more bloody pages.

Sam went into a physical and mental frenzy. "Sabotage!" he screamed, beating a fist on the desk. "I handpicked the staff myself because of their sadistic qualities!" here he strove to bend a paperclip out of Shape. "And those pigs. What do they think this place Is, the Carlton Hotel? Christ! the expense bill will be enormous!" He envisaged himself pedaling to work on a bicycle. "And you, you great twit" he bawled, belaboring Saunders about the head with his ball-pen, "Why didn't you tell me sooner so I could have caught them in the act? Be Jasus! I would have given them..." here he suddenly stopped, a thought making cold fingers play an arpeggio on his spine.

The cook!. Which cook had flagrantly broken the rules? He hoped it wasn't Miss Scringe for she was the object of his erotic day dreams in which he, Sam L'Amour, shagged the arse off her among the baked bean tins and he hoped that one day his dream would be realised.

"Who... Who was the cook?" he asked. "Miss Scringe!" croaked Saunders through the blood and pain of his beating. Sam's heart sank. How he wished it had been any of the other cooks, to whom it would have been easy to give vent his Irish fury to. But Miss Scringe! But duty, and the twenty pounds a week that went with it, called. "Send Miss Scringe to me. And who was the resident?" "Arnold, Grand Master" replied Saunders. "Right, tell him I want him outside my office. As for you, you must be punished for lacking in your duty. Your ration of carrion will be reduced for a month" "That", he said to himself with glee, "Ought to balance the bread stakes" then aloud. "Send in Miss Scringe" Suddenly, Sam caught his breath. Yes! if he played his cards right, Miss Scringe would be his! there was a timid tap on the door. "Do come in" said Sam sweetly. Miss Scringe entered. Sam's fly buttons nearly popped off with the passion that lay locked in his loins. "Now then, my dear, it has been brought to my notice that you gave one of the residents extra bread. This is very serious but I am sure we can sort things out" he smiled, laying a hand quivering with passion on the quivering mass of flesh that was her knee.

Miss Scringe, having been to bed in the last twenty years with such diverse objects as candles, cucumbers and pork sausages but never a man, promptly grabbed his hand in a judo lock and thrust it up the leg of her ex-wrac bloomers (seven and sixpence, Roy's Surplus Stores) and begged him to "'Ave 'er away". After carefully removing his hand from where it had been unexpectedly but delightfully placed and making sure he had not lost his watch in the process, Sam took off her bloomers and using them to protect the carpet, fulfilled his ambition. All that was missing were the tins of baked beans. Two minutes later he saw her to the door, promising to find her some overtime to supplement her meagre wage.

He called in Arnold and he too, noticed the pallor of the young man's cheeks and how thin he looked. He also noticed that Arnold's right eye was watery and bloodshot. "Right, Arnold, because you have violated the rules I have no option but to terminate your residence at this hostel" "If you throw me out" Arnold replied "All of Norwich will know that you were cocking the cook. I saw it all through the keyhole." Sam knew he was a beaten man. All he could do was to keep a check on Arnold, a close check on the expense sheet and a closer check still on Miss Scringe's menstrual cycle.

THE DISBELIEVER
1964

Bill Jennings was leading the two man expedition.

Carefully, he studied the terrain. "We'll have to go careful here, Fred"

A few feet behind him, Fred Hartley agreed. But to conquer Mount Everest! What an achievement!

In reality, they were climbing a bombed-out house but to two ten year old boys it was what they imagined it to be.

Having scaled the broken staircase and reached the first floor, their aim was to access the gaping hole in the roof. Bill reached up for a handhold. The brick suddenly came away, and falling from his grasp, bounced off a joist of the missing floorboards beneath them and ended up in pieces on the ground floor.

Blinking back the dust from his eyes Bill gave an opinion. "It looks dodgy, Fred, let's turn back." As well as gathering such trophies as grazed knees and clouts from their fathers for daring to enter such places, there was also the excitement of treasure hunting. On one such occasion Bill had found six pennies hidden under a mantle of lathe dust, the search culminating in a rare visit to the sweet shop.

One day, whilst sifting through a pile of bricks and plaster, Fred came across an old handbag. Opening the clasp revealed a splintered mirror and a crumpled, faded photograph of an elderly woman. "Haven't seen her around here" said Bill. "She might have been a relative who lived elsewhere" offered Fred.

Suddenly he said "Bill, do you believe in ghosts? "Course not" scoffed Bill. "Anyway, are you trying to scare me?" Fred paused, "No. But don't you sometimes wonder about the people who used to live in these places. I mean, I know that when the sirens go, people go to the air raid shelters but what about those who get killed?" "Shut up!" said Bill. "I mean" continued Fred "I wonder if they haunt their houses and.." "Pack it in!" cut in Bill, becoming aware of the suddening darkness. "Let's go home."

Later that evening in the cosy atmosphere of his mother's kitchen Bill broached the subject.

"What made you go all morbid back there?" he asked Fred. "I wasn't being morbid!" Fred flushed indignantly, "My Gran reckons that some people have something called second sight and that they can see ghosts and.." "Rubbish!" interjected Bill, reaching for a pack of cards. "Once you're dead, you're dead. The trouble with your Gran is that she's too old fashioned. Fancy a game of Rummy?"

The treasure hunting and house climbing came to an end when both boys were evacuated to Wales for the duration of the war. There, billeted in different areas, they lost touch with one another. Returning home to London when the war ended, Fred was told that Bill's house had sustained a direct hit but his family were safe in the shelter at the time and had since moved out of the district.

n due course, Fred passed out of his teens and into two years conscription in the
army, in which he joined the R.EM.E. Upon demob he became channeled into an
engineering firm, making car parts. Courtship and marriage followed and at the age of
twenty six, fatherhood.
Four years later he moved his family into 18, Kennet Grove. E.2. Fred lived life
simply but happy.
Sometime later, a FOR SALE sign appeared at number 24 but was taken down soon
after. Fred remarked upon this to his wife, Sheila. "Oh. Yes!" she exclaimed, "A
couple moved in this morning. I didn't see any children, though."
The following day Fred performed his usual Saturday ritual of washing the car down.
After checking the engine he slammed the bonnet shut, turned, and almost collided
with the new tenants of number 24. "Bill!', he cried in amazement. "Bill! How are
you?" Surprise choked further words in his throat. Bill held tight his handshake,
thoughts tumbling through his mind. All he could say was "I'm okay, Fred". The
absurdity ran through his mind "Dr. Livingstone, I presume?"

A little while later, Bill and his wife Anne were sitting in Fred's front room and over a
cup of tea relating the events which led them to take up residence at Number 24.
The two families became quite close, visiting each other and taking their holidays
together. Thursday nights were usually spent in the Hartley household watching the
television, followed afterwards by discussions on the merits or otherwise of the
evening's viewing. Sometimes, Fred and Bill regaled their wives with tales of their
childhood escapades. One Thursday evening, as a result of viewing one particular
program, Fred started a debate on ghosts "I bet that has happened to some people for
real" he opened with. "Don't tell me you still believe in ghosts!" Bill said laughingly.
"Why not!" retorted Fred. "Look at the time that newspaper published people's
experiences". "Oh.Yeah. for a fee of two pounds fifty!" Bill bantered "Have you ever
seen a ghost?" "No, I haven't" Fred replied "But that does not mean they don't exist."
The talk went back and forth until Bill reminded Fred about the incident regarding the
photo in the handbag and the subject dissolved into another of their childhood
adventures together.

Bill was polishing his shoes when the doorbell rang. "I'll get it" Anne called out.
"Come in, Fred. Bill is just getting ready." Fred went to the foot of the stairs. "Bill,"
he raised his voice, "I'm just running old Mr. Lewis and his wife down to the station
with their luggage. Their train leaves at seven so I'll see you down the pub later"
"Okay, Fred" Bill answered. "See you later on." He heard Fred's car pull away as he
came down the stairs. "I won't get too drunk, love" he quipped, giving his wife a kiss.
he smiled. He always said that, every Friday night. "Don't forget to bring me home a
Babycham" she reminded him. He never forgot.

The barman's shout interrupted the downing of his third pint. "Phone call for you, Bill" he yelled above the din. "For me?" Bill cleared his thoughts. Holding the receiver to one ear and holding his hand over the other, he strained to hear his wife's voice. "Bill, please come home. There's been..." the line went quiet. Looking down, he saw the lead had been   draped across the phone cradle and as he had turned his head to catch her words, the lead had tightened, cutting off their conversation.

"Tom", he called to the barman, "I'm off home. Something's up. Tell Fred when he comes in, I'll see him later."

As he passed number 24, he caught sight of Fred standing in the porch. He called out in recognition, "Fred, I've had a phone call from Anne. I'll see you afterwards." Fred waved back.

Reaching home, Bill fumbled with his key. Anne opened the door and threw her arms around him. "Oh! Bill!", she cried. "A stolen car smashed into Fred's as he was driving back from the station." Here she broke down and through her sobs Bill caught the words... "And he was killed."